W9-AWB-485

This book is dedicated to all who find Nature not an adversary to conquer and destroy, but a storehouse of infinite knowledge and experience linking man to all things past and present. They know conserving the natural environment is essential to our future well-being.

YELLOWSTONE

THE STORY BEHIND THE SCENERY®

by Roger Anderson and Carol Shively Anderson

Roger and Carol Shively Anderson have been career professionals with the National Park Service, serving at four different park areas since 1980. Carol currently manages interpretive services in the Lake District of Yellowstone. Roger recently left the Service to teach, write, and pursue consulting opportunities.

Yellowstone National Park, located in the northwestern corner of Wyoming, is the world's first national park. Established in 1872, it preserves unparalleled geothermal features.

Front cover: Old Faithful from Geyser Hill, photo by Salvatore Vasapolli. Inside front cover: Bull moose, photo by Art Wolfe. Page 1: Clark's nutcracker, photo by Erwin and Peggy Bauer. Page 2/3: Lower Falls of the Yellowstone River, photo by Diana L. Stratton. Page 4/5: Sunset over Midway Geyser Basin, photo by Salvatore Vasapolli.

Edited by Cheri C. Madison. Book design by K. C. DenDooven.

Twelfth Printing, 2002 • Revised Edition

YELLOWSTONE: THE STORY BEHIND THE SCENERY © 1998 KC PUBLICATIONS, INC.
"The Story Behind the Scenery"; "in pictures... The Continuing Story"; and the parallelogram forms and colors within are registered in the U.S. Patent and Trademark Office.
LC 98-65027. ISBN 0-88714-140-4.

Yellowstone is more than a place—
it's an idea. It is a testament of
the importance of wildness to the
American people, and a declaration of
their will to preserve it for future generations

Yellowstone is a place that captivated a continent, and a concept that inspired the world. It is here that the national park idea was born.

According to legend, a group of explorers, the Washburn Expedition, camped at the headwaters of the Madison River on the last night of their journey through Yellowstone. That evening around the campfire, their conversation turned to the remarkable wonders they had seen—mysterious geysers, thundering waterfalls, colorful canyons, and herds of wildlife. As they considered how these might be exploited for personal gain and profit, one among them, Cornelius Hedges, suggested a different way:

This great wilderness does not belong to us. It belongs to the nation. Let us make a public park of it and set it aside...never to be changed, but to be kept sacred always.

Some historians doubt the accuracy of this account. In fact, it is known that others conceived of this grand idea prior to this historic campfire. And yet, all cultures need legends to remind them of their best moments, and for Americans, the national park idea is one of these.

What did the early mountain men and expeditions see to inspire such thoughts? They found a land like none other. They discovered the largest

"...a thousand Yellowstone wonders are calling, Look up and down and round about you!"

JOHN MUIR, 1901

concentration of geysers in the world, and gave them such names as Giant, Grand, Castle, Grotto, Riverside, and Old Faithful to describe this incredible display of nature's fountains. They saw spectacularly colored hot springs and seething caldrons of explosive mud. They encountered the intricate travertine terraces of the Mammoth Hot Springs, tier upon tier of colorful cascading stone.

They traversed the broad wilderness of the Yellowstone Plateau, the remnants of one of the greatest volcanic eruptions in the history of time. They marveled at the world's largest petrified forest, immortalized by ancient lava flows. They came upon the largest lake at high elevation

on the continent and massive waterfalls carving a dramatic canyon, painted in nature's most brilliant hues. They crossed the high country of the Continental Divide, where many of the great North American rivers are born, including what is now the longest free-flowing river in the lower 48 states, which one day would give the park its name, the Yellowstone.

They encountered vast landscapes and an array of animals roaming free—what is today, the wildlife heritage of the nation. Here in this wild land, they found a refuge not only for wildlife, but for the human soul. You can, too.

"This Good Fire Mountain"

There are few more impressive manifestations of the power and mystery of the earth than Yellowstone. The great American poet Robert Frost once noted, "some say the world will end in fire, some say in ice." In Yellowstone, the world *began* with fire and ice and continues to be shaped by both. Here, the hidden fires within the earth have expressed themselves through the ages to celebrate some of the most diverse and dramatic landscapes ever assembled in any one place. Whether it be in the great geyser basins of Old Faithful or Norris, the Grand Canyon, Mammoth Hot Springs, the glacial valley of Lamar, or the expansive Yellowstone Lake bounded by the ancient Absaroka range—in all, the internal forces of the earth reach the surface to reveal another page in yet another chapter in the amazing geologic story that is Yellowstone.

First and foremost, Yellowstone is a geologic park. Geology is the foundation upon which all plant and animal life exists, and it is the stage on which the human drama unfolds. When the first exploring parties surveyed the Yellowstone territory, they were impressed by many of the sights they encountered—the wildlife, mountain scenery, and fast-flowing headwaters of the region. However, none captured their imagination more than the geologic wonders they found here. The "natural curiosities" of the geysers, hot springs, mudpots, and fumaroles inspired members of these early expeditions, and it is primarily for these treasures that Yellowstone was ultimately set apart as the world's first national park in 1872.

Yellowstone is the site of some of the largest volcanic eruptions in history—a display of the power and potential lying beneath the earth's surface. Today, this power is manifested in a myriad of geothermal features, the likes of which are found nowhere else on the planet. Combine this tale with ancient seas and mountain building, petrified forests, and continued volcanic uplift and you have what many regard as geologically the most interesting place in the world.

THE YELLOWSTONE HOTSPOT

At the center of Yellowstone's geologic story is the Yellowstone Plateau. "This good fire moun-

ED COOPER

Overlooking Lamar Valley, the petrified trees perched atop Specimen Ridge reveal ancient geologic tales of volcanic eruptions and the life preserved in their aftermath. Formed 50 million years ago, these stories in stone tell of a time when a warmer climate reigned and trees such as redwoods were found in the park.

ED COOPER

The Yellowstone River begins its 671-mile journey to the Missouri in the southern mountains of the park. Along the way, this mighty river carves some of the most dramatic scenery in Yellowstone. Near Tower Fall, the erosional power of water is fully revealed in the steep spires and pinnacles for which the fall is named.

tain," as naturalist John Muir called it, is a large volcanic plateau that dominates the Yellowstone landscape. Situated at about 8,000 feet, it is a vast wilderness, encompassing over 1,000 square miles, characterized by a rolling terrain of lava flows, whose poor volcanic soils yield thick forests of lodgepole pine, the park's most prolific tree.

This broad plateau lies in the heart of the northern Rocky Mountains. It also lies at the very heart of our story. Here, powerful volcanic forces erupted 2 million, 1.3 million, and as recently as 600,000 years ago to create three of the world's largest volcanic depressions, or calderas.

Like the Hawaiian islands, Yellowstone owes its origins to a geologic "hotspot" of molten rock,

7

ED COOPER

Just outside the caldera rim near Madison Junction, Tuff Cliff exposes welded ash flows of rhyolite that were laid down during the volcanic eruption 600,000 years ago. Hot particles of volcanic ash compacted together to create a dense layer of rock called welded tuff.

or magma. Hotspots are found throughout the world, mostly underlying the thin crust of the ocean floors. Continental hotspots, like that found under Yellowstone, however, are a rarity in nature. On continents, the crust of the earth is typically 25 to 30 miles thick, below which is found the hot molten material of the earth's mantle. Yellowstone is the exception. It is believed that a plume of magma rises through the mantle into the crust where it forms a shallow magma chamber near the earth's surface, perhaps as little as 1 to 3 miles beneath Yellowstone.

This hotspot of magma set the stage as the North American Plate, or continental crust, moved southwestward over the stationary hotspot, like a sheet of paper moving over a burning candle. Emerging from Idaho's Snake River Plain, the hotspot burst onto the face of the Yellowstone landscape beginning about 2 million years ago in what is considered the largest volcanic eruption ever recorded in the history of the earth. As the continental crust continued its slide in a southwesterly direction, the center of volcanic activity slowly shifted in the opposite direction, trending toward the northeast and further into the Yellowstone region. The result is a series of three calderas tracking from beyond the park's southwest boundary on a line to the northeast through the center of the park.

Occurring at approximately 600,000-year intervals, the second volcano exploded about 1.3 million years ago, just outside the park's southwest boundary in the area of Island Park, Idaho.

SALVATORE VASAPOLLI

Although small in comparison to the other eruptions, it still ranks among the greatest volcanic episodes in history.

Centered under the park, the last and most recent volcano erupted about 600,000 years ago, setting the stage for the story of Yellowstone today. The result was dramatic and catastrophic. Imagine during this time, magma rising from deep within the earth, ascending toward the surface, and accumulating in the upper reaches of the earth's crust. As it does, the ground above the magma chamber stretches and expands, becoming thinner and thinner as it is forced upward in a doming effect, much like a blister forming on the earth's surface. Ultimately, as the continual uplift caused by the rising magma expands across an extensive land area, "ring fractures" or concentric cracks begin to form around the base of the dome, like the circular cracks in a pie crust as it heats and rises. These cracks then spread down toward the magma chamber. When they breached this highly pressurized chamber, they set in motion yet another of the world's largest volcanic explosions.

The volcano roared to life with terrific force, blasting phenomenal quantities of hot molten rock, ash, and gases upward and outward in a large cataclysmic event. In total, over 240 cubic miles of volcanic material erupted, an explosion approximately 1,000 times more powerful than Mount Saint Helens in 1980. Volcanic ash flows spewed forth from the ring fractures at temperatures in excess of 1500°F, spreading across thousands of square miles of land in a matter of moments, destroying all life in its wake. Likewise, ash and dust flew across much of North America, clouding the skies and most likely affecting the world's weather patterns in profound ways.

As volcanic debris continued to erupt from the earth, the upper portion of the magma chamber emptied. In this void, with nothing left to hold up the roof of the chamber, a great collapse occurred as the ground slumped and caved in on itself along the ring fractures, giving birth to the present-day Yellowstone caldera. In forming the caldera, the overlying mountain ranges and other

JOHN P. GEORGE

Immense lava flows of rhyolite spilled from the caldera to form the rolling terrain of the present-day Yellowstone Plateau. The silica in these rhyolite boulders is instrumental in the formation of the pressure-tight plumbing system that enables the great geysers of Yellowstone.

For most visitors to Yellowstone, trying to visualize this giant caldera is a challenging task, partly because it is so big, but also because younger lava flows have masked its appearance. Shortly after the collapse of the magma chamber roof, more magma resurged in two areas within the caldera, doming the earth near Old Faithful and also north of Yellowstone Lake near LeHardy Rapids. Almost immediately after the formation of the caldera, magma rose from this renewed chamber, flowing quietly out of the earth as a type of lava known as rhyolite. These intermittent flows of rhyolite oozed from the magma chamber until about 70,000 years ago. They filled in and covered much of the caldera basin, burying most of its rim in the process and giving rise to the Yellowstone Plateau.

WHAT OF THE FUTURE?

With volcanoes erupting approximately every 600,000 years, is Yellowstone poised for another massive explosion? Once again, evidence points to a shallow magma chamber just beneath Yellowstone in the northeast portion of the present caldera. Uplift, often associated with rising magma, has been recorded in this area, most notably at the LeHardy Rapids on the Yellowstone River, north of Yellowstone Lake. Over a 50-year period ending in 1985, benchmarks have revealed

surface landforms were either blown away by the erupting volcano or consumed in the collapse of the caldera.

Today's caldera is immense. Measuring approximately 47 miles long and 28 miles wide, this huge volcanic depression likely reached several thousand feet deep at the time of its formation. Why then, many may wonder when traveling through Yellowstone, is such an obvious crater in the earth not readily apparent? The answer lies in two words—lava flows.

Throughout most of the Yellowstone Plateau, the caldera rim has been buried by subsequent flows of lava. Lewis Falls is one of the few places where the actual rim is exposed at the surface, with its waters flowing over the edge of the caldera. The other point where the rim is clearly observable is Gibbon Falls, along the road between Norris and Madison.

Aptly named for the Roman goddess of artists and sculptors, Minerva Spring illustrates the delicate terracing that characterizes the features of Mammoth Hot Springs. Always a work in progress, these fountains can lay down several feet of new rock, called travertine, *in a year. The terraces at Mammoth have changed considerably since the discovery of the park. How will Minerva look on your next visit?*

that the ground here has risen a total of three feet, at a rate of approximately one half-inch per year. Is the magma chamber once again on the rise and the earth doming in preparation for a fourth eruption? In contrast, since 1985, the earth here has experienced a period of sinking, or subsidence, also at the rate of half an inch per year. Perhaps then, a volcanic episode is not on the horizon—or maybe the earth is just catching its breath as it prepares for the creation of the next Yellowstone caldera.

One thing is certain: regardless of what happens in the future, much of Yellowstone's breathtaking scenery today owes its origins to this recent volcanic past. Yellowstone Lake lies in a basin bounded by the rim of the 600,000-year-old caldera to the east and subsequent flows of lava to the west. Recent underwater explorations of the lake have revealed deep canyons along with geysers, hot springs, and as-

sociated thermal activity on the bottom of this big cold mountain lake. Lying in the heart of the park, Yellowstone Lake characterizes the beauty of a landscape that has emerged in stark contrast to the violent volcanic activity of the last 2 million years. Perhaps too, beneath the still waters of this grand lake, are hidden clues to Yellowstone's potentially explosive future. Over the next 100,000 years, time will tell.

STORIES IN STONE

Surrounding the Yellowstone caldera are stories of more ancient times that yield remarkable geologic treasures. The oldest rock revealed in Yellowstone dates back 2.7 billion years in the northern mountains of the park, exposing here the very foundation of North America. Later, 500 million years ago, Yellowstone was a far different place than it is today. Covered by shallow inland

SCOTT T. SMITH

FRED HIRSCHMANN

The rugged Absaroka Mountain Range provides a formidable geographic barrier along the park's eastern boundary. This range is named for the Crow Indians who called themselves Absaroka, *which has been interpreted to mean "children of the large-beaked bird." Truly a terrain of fire and ice, these mountains formed about 50 million years ago from erupting volcanoes during an active period of mountain building in the Rocky Mountains. Through the ages, glaciers have continued to scour and sculpt these peaks. Some of the most impressive high country in the park, the Absarokas remain snowcapped most of the summer.*

seas, ocean sediments built up layer upon layer to form the common sedimentary rocks found in the park—limestone, sandstone, and shale. Today, these marine deposits are found at Mammoth Hot Springs in the limestone formations issuing from the ephemeral hot springs there, and also in the rugged sandstone blocks used nearby in the construction of historic Fort Yellowstone.

Standing in one place at Mammoth, one can see, at the same time, some of the oldest and newest rocks on earth. The park's geologic chronology spans much of the earth's history, beginning with some of the oldest rocks from the basement of time and ending just moments ago with the latest deposits of travertine on the terraces of Mammoth Hot Springs.

Between the time of ancient seas and the caldera-forming volcanoes of the recent past, a great period of mountain building began as the North American Plate collided with the Pacific Plate 100 to 50 million years ago. A time of tremendous upheaval, this powerful tectonic activity folded, faulted, and compressed the earth,

leading to the uplift and creation of the Rocky Mountain chain.

In this unstable landscape, even more ancient volcanoes arose about 50 million years ago to form the Absaroka and Washburn mountains. Lying across Yellowstone Lake and bounding the park's east side, the Absarokas are an imposing mountain range that formed from erupting volcanoes over a 15-million-year period. Today, they provide a majestic backdrop to the waters of Yellowstone Lake. At the time of their creation, they erupted silica-rich lava and ash which mixed with water to form mudflows. These mudflows surrounded and immortalized redwoods, sycamores, magnolias, dogwoods, and other trees in the world's largest petrified forest, preserving the fossil record of an earlier and warmer climatic period. These petrified forests were immortalized in myth as well, first through Native American legend and later in the early 1800s by mountain men like Jim Bridger. Today, these forests of stone can best be explored on Specimen Ridge near Lamar Valley.

W. PERRY CONWAY

FIRE AND ICE

Yellowstone is a land of contrasts and extremes. Just as the internal fires of the earth bring boiling water to the surface as geysers and hot springs, the park's high elevation and northern latitude make it also a land of deep snows and long winters. When more snow falls in winter than can melt in summer, ice begins to form under the weight of the snow and eventually begins to flow as a glacier. Though there are no active glaciers in Yellowstone today, such conditions have occurred here intermittently over the last 2 million years.

Like any good sculptor working in stone, these giant glaciers left their imprint on Yellowstone in many ways, both subtle and harsh. The region's most recent period of glaciation began about 50,000 years ago in the high mountains of the Absaroka-Beartooth Wilderness, northeast of Yellowstone. With time, vast sheets of ice, thousands of feet thick, flowed from the mountains to converge over Yellowstone Lake, covering the Yellowstone Plateau and virtually all of the park and surrounding area. While thermal basins continued to seethe beneath the ice, this land of fire and brimstone was in a deep freeze for thousands of years. At the height of this glacial era, roughly 25,000 years ago, prominent peaks like Mount Washburn and Mount Sheridan were buried underneath an icy blanket, while probably only the thin ridgeline of the Absaroka Mountains peeked above this unrelenting sea of ice. For thousands of years, ice flowed in all directions carving, scouring, and sculpting the land.

As the ice age slowly ended nearly 15,000 years ago, it left behind ample evidence of the transforming power of ice. Among the broad hills and benches of Hayden Valley, lake sediments of silt, sand, and gravel, covered in glacial till, remain from a time when the valley was filled by an ancient lake formed by an early ice dam. Large river valleys like the Firehole, Madison, and Lamar were broadened and scoured by accompanying rivers of ice. Retreating glaciers and their meltwaters gradually dropped their load of rock debris. Having carried massive stones from high, distant mountains like the Beartooths, they

Amid the long golden rays of a summer sunset, steam lofting from the crater of Great Fountain Geyser offers a reminder of the internal fires lurking within the earth.

Beneath the towering peaks of the Continental Divide lies Yellowstone Lake, the largest lake at high elevation in North America. It's a lake of many moods. In the afternoon, the wind whips it into a frothing fury—but in the morning and early evening, it's the perfect place to reflect on the peace and beauty preserved in Yellowstone.

ED COOPER

left behind fields dotted with large granite boulders, called *glacial erratics*, at places where granite is not found, like Canyon's Inspiration Point and near Lamar Valley. Glacial ponds, striated hillsides, chiseled peaks, and polished mountain faces, all fashioned by the hand of ice, create some of the finishing touches on the spectacular landscape we see today.

"Beyond the Reach of Human Art"

Nowhere else have the combined powers of fire and ice come together to create so beautiful and so sublime a work of nature as the Grand Canyon of the Yellowstone. This deep colorful canyon of many hues and moods has been cele-

During the last ice age, glaciers carried large granite boulders from their origin in the far-off Beartooth Mountains to the valleys below. As the ice sheets melted, these glacial erratics were scattered across the landscape. Today, they give testimony to the sheer power of ice.

brated in paintings and in photographs since the time it was first captured on canvas by landscape painter Thomas Moran. Even so, just as Moran described the canyon as being "beyond the reach of human art," the story of this magnificent part of Yellowstone remains somewhat beyond the reach of human understanding.

This stunning display of nature's handiwork began when the last volcano laid down rhyolitic lava flows shortly after the caldera's collapse. In carving the canyon, the Yellowstone River was first aided by the action of a geyser basin that formed within the lava flow. The hot water, steam, and gases of these thermal features hydrothermally altered the normally hard rhyolite, weakening the rock and making it susceptible to erosion and further downcutting by the river. Later, it is believed that glaciers assisted in the carving of the canyon, not by the brute force of ice, but through the release of torrential flood waters from melting ice dams near Yellowstone Lake. This huge volume of water flowing through the soft canyon rock further eroded and defined the present appearance of the canyon.

Today, remnants of the area's thermal activity are still visible within the canyon. Through the years, the chemical alteration of the rhyolite due to these hot waters has caused a variety of iron compounds in the rock to oxidize, or rust, creating a palette of yellow, red, and orange colors on the canyon walls. Perhaps Thomas Moran had it right, for as an early visitor noted, "no artist could paint or imitate the wonderful colorings, the rugged grandeur of the walls and the sublime nature of the whole scene."

ED COOPER

Sitting astride the Continental Divide, Yellowstone preserves some of the most pristine headwaters of the nation. Each year, snows from the park's long winters melt in a torrent of spring runoff, flushing out river systems, carving the landscape, and providing an abundance of water to lower elevations.

SUGGESTED READING AND VIDEOS

BROCK, THOMAS D. *Life at High Temperatures*. Yellowstone National Park, Wyoming: Yellowstone Association for Natural Science, History & Education, Inc., 1994.

COTTRELL, DR. WILLIAM H. *Born of Fire: The Volcanic Origin of Yellowstone National Park*. Boulder, Colorado: Roberts Rinehart, Inc. Publishers, 1987.

EHRLICH, GRETEL. *Yellowstone: Land of Fire and Ice*. New York, New York: HarperCollins West, 1995.

FRITZ, WILLIAM J. *Roadside Geology of the Yellowstone Country*. Missoula, Montana: Mountain Press Publishing Company, 1985.

GOOD, JOHN M. and KENNETH L. PIERCE. *Interpreting the Landscapes of Grand Teton and Yellowstone National Parks: Recent and Ongoing Geology*. Moose, Wyoming: Grand Teton Natural History Association, 1996.

Yellowstone: Imprints of Geologic Time. Produced, written, and filmed by Blair Robbins. Seattle, Washington: Terra Productions.

SALVATORE VASAPOLLI

The power of water and its ability to carve canyons is never more in evidence than at the brink of the Lower Falls of the Yellowstone River. The force of the water, as it rushes over the precipice to form one of the park's tallest waterfalls, is revealed downstream in the colorful walls of the Grand Canyon of the Yellowstone.

Nature's Rarest Fountains

JOHN P. GEORGE

With its erupting waters arcing across the Firehole River, Riverside Geyser is among the most predictable and popular geysers in Yellowstone. Its ideal setting, amid a grassy meadow at the river's edge, makes it the perfect spot for an afternoon picnic while awaiting the next eruption. Those who wait are often rewarded with a rainbow in the mist of the geyser's spray.

With half of the earth's geothermal features, Yellowstone holds the planet's most diverse and intact collection of geysers, hot springs, mudpots, and fumaroles. Its more than 300 geysers make up two thirds of all those found on earth. Combine this with over 10,000 thermal features comprised of brilliantly colored hot springs, bubbling mudpots, and steaming fumaroles, and you have a place like no other. Geyserland, fairyland, wonderland—through the years, all have been used to describe the natural wonder and magic of this unique land.

Yellowstone's vast collection of thermal features are a constant reminder of the park's recent volcanic past. Indeed, the caldera provides the setting that allows such features as Old Faithful to exist and in such great numbers.

COLORFUL CAVERNS

In the high mountains surrounding the Yellowstone Plateau, water falls as snow or rain and slowly percolates through layers of porous rock, amid cracks and fissures in the earth's crust created by the ring fracturing and collapse of the caldera. Sinking to a depth of nearly 10,000 feet, this cold water comes into contact with the hot rocks associated with the shallow magma chamber beneath the park. As the water is heated, its temperatures rise well above the boiling point to become superheated. This superheated water, however, remains in a liquid state due to the great pressure and weight pushing down on it from overlying rock and water. The result is something akin to a giant pressure cooker, with water temperatures in excess of 400°F.

The highly energized water is less dense than the colder, heavier water sinking around it. This creates convection currents that allow the lighter, more buoyant, superheated water to begin its slow arduous journey back toward the surface through rhyolitic lava flows, following

The Upper Geyser Basin is home to the largest concentration of geysers in the world. Sawmill Geyser, in the foreground, plays often throughout the day. A fountain-type geyser, Sawmill resembles a hot spring with its open crater that fills with hot water during eruptions. The other kind of geyser is the cone-type, best illustrated in the massive cone formation of Castle Geyser, erupting in the distance.

the cracks, fissures, and weak areas of the earth's crust. Rhyolite is essential to geysers because it contains an abundance of silica, the mineral from which glass is made. As the hot water travels through this "natural plumbing system," the high temperatures dissolve some of the silica in the rhyolite, yielding a solution of silica-rich water.

At the surface, these silica-laden waters form a rock called *geyserite*, or *sinter*, creating the massive geyser cones, the scalloped edges of hot springs, and the expansive light-colored barren surface characteristic of geyser basins. While in solution underground, some of this silica deposits as geyserite on the walls of the plumbing system forming a pressure-tight seal, locking in the hot water and creating a system that can withstand the great pressure needed to produce a geyser.

With the rise of superheated water through this complex plumbing system, the immense pressure exerted over the water drops as it nears the surface. The heat energy, if released in a slow steady manner, gives rise to a hot spring, the most abundant and colorful thermal feature in the park.

The elegant formations around the hot springs demonstrate the artistry of nature in the geyser basins. As the mineral-laden waters begin to cool at the surface, the silica in the water is deposited to form geyserite, *creating the cones of geysers and the delicate scalloping at the edge of many hot springs.*

FRED HIRSCHMANN

ED COOPER

Morning Glory Pool, near Old Faithful, is one of Yellowstone's best-known hot springs because the road once passed by it. But popularity has a price. Its once-bright colors have been diminished by the many coins thrown in it. Still, Morning Glory remains one of the park's most lovely springs.

Hot springs with names like Morning Glory, Grand Prismatic, Abyss, Emerald, and Sapphire, are scattered like glistening jewels in a host of colors across the park's harsh volcanic plain.

Writing in 1871, early explorer Dr. Ferdinand Hayden captured the essence of Yellowstone's startling array of hot springs with these words:

> *Nothing ever conceived by human art could equal the peculiar vividness and delicacy of coloring of these remarkable prismatic springs....Life becomes a privilege and a blessing after one has seen and thoroughly felt these incomparable types of nature's cunning skill.*

FRED HIRSCHMANN

This small but intriguing geyser cone at the bottom of the Canyon is similar to the thermal features that originally aided in the creation of this colorful chasm.

Grand Prismatic Spring at Midway Geyser Basin is the largest hot spring in the park. It is so big that it can only be fully appreciated in aerial photographs. The brilliant yellows and oranges around the perimeter of the pool are a result of the bacteria which grow in it. Each color represents a different type of bacteria specialized to survive at a certain range of hot temperatures.

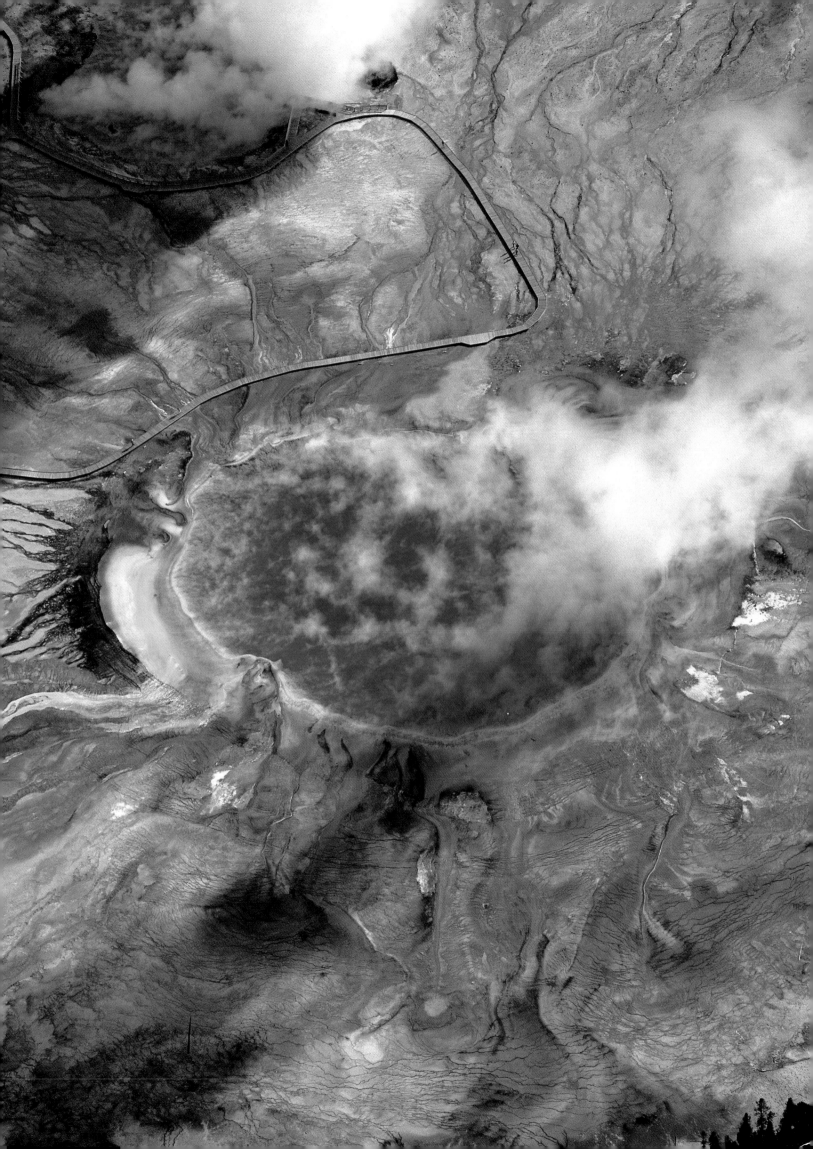

Among the most intriguing of all thermal features are the mysterious caldrons known as mudpots. The Fountain Paint Pot area contains all four kinds of thermal features: gurgling mudpots, colorful hot springs, steaming fumaroles, and active geysers.

RUSS FINLEY

Despite their intriguing bubbles, most mudpots are not actually boiling. The explosive action is due to gases—steam, carbon dioxide, and hydrogen sulfide—erupting through the viscous mud. It is the hydrogen sulfide which gives these features their distinctive sulfuric aroma.

FRED HIRSCHMANN

MUDPOTS AND FUMAROLES

Where hot water is limited and hydrogen sulfide gas is present (emitting the "rotten egg" smell common to thermal areas), sulfuric acid is generated. The acid dissolves the surrounding rock into fine particles of silica and clay which mix with what little water there is to form the seething and bubbling mudpots. The sights, sounds, and smells of areas like Artist and Fountain Paint Pots and Mud Volcano, make these curious features some of the most memorable in the park. Fumaroles, or steam vents, are hot springs with a lot of heat, but so little water that it all boils away before reaching the surface. The result is a loud hissing vent of steam and gases, which can be found in nearly all thermal areas.

FRED HIRSCHMANN

In acidic features, color can be the result of mineral content. Here in the backcountry, iron oxides create the rusty red color. Unofficially known as Tomato Soup Pool, this feature is also a good example of how the only constant in nature is change. Tomato Soup Pool is no longer red.

JOHN P. GEORGE

During the stagecoach days in Yellowstone, early park visitors often wrote in their journals of this remarkable mountain that roared. Between Mammoth Hot Springs and Norris Geyser Basin, Roaring Mountain was covered with hissing fumaroles or steam vents which thundered with great volume. Today, these fumaroles are not as vocal as they once were. They still send plumes of steam into the sky, however, creating an impressive sight—especially on a crisp fall morning or during the winter when the air temperature can be over 200 degrees lower than that of the steam.

21

"A Frozen Waterfall"

At Mammoth Hot Springs, a rarer kind of spring is born when the hot water ascends through the ancient limestone deposits of the area, instead of the silica-rich lava flows common elsewhere in the park. The results are strikingly different and unique. They invoke a landscape that resembles a cave turned inside out, with its delicate features exposed for all to see. The flowing waters spill across the surface to sculpt magnificent travertine limestone terraces. As one early visitor described them, "no human architect ever designed such intricate fountains as these. The water trickles over the edges from one to another, blending them together with the effect of a frozen waterfall."

The Great Geysers

Sprinkled amid the hot springs are the rarest fountains of all, the geysers. What makes them rare and distinguishes them from hot springs is that somewhere, usually near the surface in the plumbing system of a geyser, there are one or more constrictions. Expanding steam bubbles generated from the rising hot water build up behind these constrictions, ultimately squeezing through the narrow passageways and forcing the water above to overflow from the geyser. The release of water at the surface prompts a sudden decline in pressure of the hotter waters at great depth, triggering a violent chain reaction of tremendous steam explosions in which the volume of rising, now boiling, water expands 1,500 times or more. This expanding body of boiling superheated water bursts into the sky as one of Yellowstone's many geysers.

There are more geysers here than anywhere on earth. Old Faithful, certainly the most famous geyser, is joined by numerous others big and small, named and unnamed. Though born of the same water and rock, what is enchanting is how differently they play in the sky. Riverside Geyser shoots at an angle across the Firehole River, often forming a rainbow in its mist. Castle erupts from a cone shaped like the ruins of some medieval fortress. Grand explodes in a series of powerful bursts, towering above the surrounding trees. Echinus spouts up and out to all sides like a fireworks display of water. And Steamboat, the largest in the world, pulsates like a massive steam engine in its rare, but memorable eruptions, reaching heights of 300 to 400 feet.

TRAVERTINE FORMATIONS

WATER SEEPAGE

RISING CARBONIC ACID

LIMESTONE LAYERS

HEATED WATER

MAGMA CHAMBER

ANATOMY OF A LIMESTONE HOT SPRING

At Mammoth Hot Springs rain or melted snow sinks deep into the earth, perhaps as much as two miles, through porous rock layers and cracks in the earth's crust. At that depth the water, under great pressure from its own weight, encounters rock that has been heated by the underlying partially molten rock that lies a few miles below much of Yellowstone's surface. The water is heated far above the normal surface boiling point, and convection currents force it back to the surface through other cracks. It also absorbs volcanic gases, principally carbon dioxide, and becomes "carbonated" water, a weak carbonic-acid solution. The rising water passes through layers of limestone, dissolving some in the hot carbonic acid. But the water cools on its way up and can no longer hold as much material in solution. At the surface, then, the carbon dioxide is released into the air, and the dissolved limestone is precipitated as the *travertine* that makes up Terrace Mountain and the fanciful formations of the hot-spring terraces. Over two tons of travertine are deposited here by rising waters each day.

JEFF GNASS

Bubbling, gurgling, spraying, and jetting, these unique displays of nature which spout and dance across the Yellowstone landscape, inspired naturalist John Muir to write of them:

So numerous are they and varied, nature seems to have gathered them from all over the world as specimens of her rarest fountains to show in one place what she can do.

SUGGESTED READING AND VIDEOS

BRYAN, T. SCOTT. *The Geysers of Yellowstone.* Niwot, Colorado: University Press of Colorado, 1995.
BRYAN, T. SCOTT. *Geysers: What They Are and How They Work.* Boulder, Colorado: Roberts Rinehart, Inc. Publishers, 1990.

Geysers of Yellowstone. Written, photographed, and edited by Russ Finley. Whittier, California: Finley-Holiday Film Corp.

The ethereal beauty of Canary Spring is magnified by the soft colors of the sunrise. Mammoth is the only place in the park where this type of hot spring can be found. These intricate features of travertine are powered by the same underground forces as the geysers, but the hot water works its way up through limestone rather than rhyolite, resulting in these delicate fountains.

Overleaf: Hot and cold water mix as the aptly named Firehole River meanders through the Upper, Midway, and Lower Geyser Basins, receiving runoff from geysers and hot springs along the way. Photo by Salvatore Vasapolli.

ALAN & SANDY CAREY

Wildlife and Wildlands

Yellowstone preserves the wildlife heritage of the nation. From its snowy peaks to its broad valleys, it captures the essence of what the American West once was, before being tamed by the human hand. Often called the American Serengeti, the park lies at the center of the largest temperate ecosystem in the world, its premier habitat protecting many of the great wildlife species of the continent.

This is the magic of Yellowstone. People from around the world come here every year, and as they venture through this wild land, there is the quiet anticipation that they may see a herd of elk or buffalo, or the unspoken hope that they might catch a glimpse of a grizzly bear in the early morning light. Yellowstone's vast wilderness of forests, valleys, rivers, and lakes is nature's Eden.

On his visit to the park in 1885, naturalist John Muir described Yellowstone with these words:

> *It is a big wholesome wilderness on the broad summit of the Rocky Mountains, favored with abundance of rain and snow,...where the greatest of the American rivers take their rise. The central portion is a densely forested and comparatively level volcanic plateau with an average elevation of about eight thousand feet above the sea...unnumbered lakes shine in it, united by a famous band of streams that rush up out of lava beds, or fall from the frosty peaks...to the main rivers, singing cheerily on through every difficulty, cunningly dividing and finding their way east and west to the two far off seas.*

Muir's description still holds true today. The park is dominated by dense lodgepole pine forests, which carpet the rolling lava flows of the Yellowstone Plateau. Occasional stands of spruce

SCOTT T. SMITH

A lone bison rests in a lodgepole forest that burned during 1988. Large animals like bison and elk have benefited greatly from the improved habitat resulting from the fires. The burned forests have given way to an abundance of new grasses, diversifying the habitat for these grazing animals.

Great efforts are being made to save the magnificent, yet threatened, grizzly bear. Its fate will ultimately be an indicator of the commitment of humanity to preserve another species for future generations.

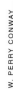
BOB ZELLAR/J-R AGENCY AT RIVERBEND

W. PERRY CONWAY

This fleet-footed animal, the pronghorn antelope, is commonly seen in the sagebrush lowlands of the northern part of the park, often near the Roosevelt Arch at the north entrance. Its natural camouflage makes it difficult to see until it moves, and quickly, up to 60 miles per hour.

and fir trees are found where fire has not interrupted the march from pioneer to climax species. The northern tier of the park, known as "the northern range," is characterized by sagebrush grasslands and Douglas fir forests, splashed with stands of aspen. Several expansive valleys—the Hayden, Lamar, Pelican, and Firehole—were left in the wake of the glaciers. Small areas of high desert and alpine tundra cling to the mountain-

JAMES TALLON

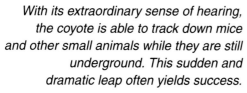

With its extraordinary sense of hearing, the coyote is able to track down mice and other small animals while they are still underground. This sudden and dramatic leap often yields success.

This impressive clashing of horns is not a fight to the finish, but more a posturing for dominance. Bighorn sheep have a pocket of air in the skull behind the forehead to cushion the blows sustained during this rutting ritual. As with all horned animals, both the males and females wear horns for a lifetime, though the male's are larger with the distinctive curl. For animals with antlers, like moose and elk, only the males have racks, which they shed each year.

tops. Water-loving willows and cottonwoods line the marshy wetlands of the park's many lakes, rivers, and streams, whose waters run toward one side of the country or the other, depending on which side of the Continental Divide they flow.

THE HABITAT CONNECTION

"Where can I see wildlife?" is a common question among visitors to the park. To understand wildlife, one must understand their habitat. Habitat provides everything a plant or animal needs to survive—food, water, shelter, and space. The words *flora* and *fauna* are necessarily linked together.

For example, one will find the exotic-looking pronghorn antelope in the sagebrush grasslands because sagebrush is its primary food. With little forest cover in which to hide, the pronghorn (not a true antelope) has evolved to be the fastest land mammal in North America, reaching speeds up to 60 miles per hour.

At the other extreme, one may find the appropriately named bighorn sheep on the towering rocky outcrops of the alpine tundra and the high desert. Extraordinary climbers, they can outmaneuver most predators with their swift surefootedness. In the fall, as the males compete with each other for the females during the *rut*, or

mating season, the sound of horns clashing rings through the canyons of the high country.

It is often hard to look past the herds of bison and elk to see the smaller mammals in the open valleys of Yellowstone. But an attempt to do so will be rewarded. Cloaked in stealthy gray and brown camouflage and standing silent and still, one might not see the coyote listening closely for the sound of voles and gophers moving underground. That is, until it suddenly leaps and pounces, pulling up its wriggling prey. The coyote is everywhere, unlike his canine brothers and sisters, the red fox and gray wolf, and his feline cousins, the bobcat, lynx, and mountain lion, who are seen only occasionally. Coyote, the trickster in Indian legend, was clever enough to outlast deliberate human attempts to destroy all predators in the park. Others were not so lucky.

Like anglers, even bald eagles occasionally miss their mark. This is the one that got away. The eagle is a success story of the Endangered Species Act. Because of efforts to restore the population, they have gone from being endangered to only threatened. The survival of the national symbol is now more assured.

ALAN & SANDY CAREY

WATER WILDERNESS

The strong and massive moose has few enemies as it calmly meanders through the marshy wetlands along Yellowstone's rivers and lakes. Moose forage mostly on the willows which grow near water, but should the plants on the bottom of the river look appetizing, they may submerge completely, swimming underwater, even with a full rack of antlers, which can weigh up to 80 pounds.

The moose shares this water wilderness with many other animals. Trumpeter swans glide gracefully upstream. They may be followed by their dusky gray colored young, called *cygnets*, though this is somewhat rare. Trumpeters nest on the ground, making their offspring highly vulnerable

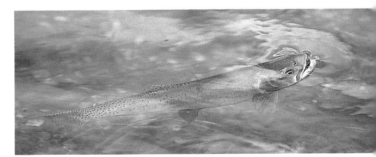

The native cutthroat trout is named for the red gash-like stripe on its neck. This fish also displays the bright red markings near its gills that occur during the springtime spawn. Over 40 species of wildlife depend on the cutthroat, now imperiled in Yellowstone Lake.

CAROL POLICH

Spring is a time of birth and new life for bison, elk, and moose. Moose calves are born in late May and early June. Seemingly all legs at birth, the awkward-looking moose calf depends on its mother during the first year of its life. In this time, she will protect it, nourish it, and teach it the skills it needs to survive. The female or "cow" moose is a formidable opponent to any predator that may threaten her young.

to predators. Overhead, the bald eagle soars downriver, hoping to snatch a fish from the surface of the water. It may take part in aerial dogfights, trying to steal a fish from the osprey, a much more adept hunter, who is able to dive deeper in the river to catch its prey. But the best fishers by far are the American white pelicans who confidently navigate the Yellowstone River in groups like flotillas of ships, gathering in a circle to fish. Rocking back and forth to herd fish into the ring, they all dive at once, as if on cue, and come up with the prize—the native Yellowstone cutthroat trout. Pelicans pull out more fish than do humans from these blue-ribbon trout streams.

The central character in this drama is the cutthroat trout. Yellowstone Lake is home to the largest inland native cutthroat trout population in the world. Dozens of other species depend on this one fish, most notably the eagle, osprey, pelican, otter, and the grizzly bear. In 1994, a larger, nonnative fish, the lake trout, was discovered in Yellowstone Lake. It is believed that this intruder was illegally introduced some years earlier. Preying on the cutthroat, the lake trout threatens to topple the fragile lake ecosystem by reducing the cutthroat trout, the one species upon which much of the lake ecology depends.

This situation illustrates the danger of introducing exotics into a native system. The demise of the cutthroat would have a dramatic impact on many other animals. As John Muir once observed, "When we try to pick out anything by itself, we find it hitched to everything else in the Universe."

THE LAST STRONGHOLD

In all, Yellowstone has over 300 species of animals, including 60 mammals, 18 fish, 4 amphibians, 5 reptiles, and more than 225 species of birds. The park is one of the last strongholds for several threatened and endangered species as well—the grizzly bear, the American bald eagle, the gray wolf, the peregrine falcon, and the whooping crane. It is also home to the largest concentration of elk in the world and some of North America's greatest herds of bison and deer.

The United Nations has proclaimed Yellowstone both a Biosphere Reserve and a World Heritage Site, acknowledging the international significance of its resources and the importance of the national park idea in the world today. Many of the landmark decisions in the history of natural resource management occurred here. The story of Yellowstone's wildlife is the story of how this idea has evolved through time.

JEFF & ALEXA HENRY

ROBERT H. SMITH/J-R AGENCY AT RIVERBEND

The difference between bison and buffalo is a matter of semantics. "Bison" is the scientific name, and "buffalo" is the common name. Early explorers thought this animal, though technically not a buffalo, resembled the Asian and African water buffalo and gave it that name. The names are now used interchangeably.

WHERE THE BUFFALO ROAM

Driving through Yellowstone's Hayden and Lamar valleys, one is likely to see herds of bison grazing peacefully on grasses and sedges. They are common enough that visitors may even become so accustomed to seeing them, the thought could cross their minds, "Just another buffalo." If they only knew that this could well have been the place where it was said, "This is where the last bison in the wild perished forever." It is probably

FRED HIRSCHMANN

Bison are survivors. They survived extinction when other ancient animals like the woolly mammoth did not. They also survived the brush with extinction that came with the settling of the American West. Like their ancestors, each year these bison survive the challenge of winter in the high country. Bison are built for winter. The huge muscle in their shoulders enables them to plow through deep snows. Their thick fur insulates them from sub-zero temperatures. If there were only one word to characterize the bison, it would be "perseverance."

no coincidence that the bison appears on the arrowhead symbol of the National Park Service, because this animal and its story symbolize the national park idea itself.

By the turn of the century, the great bison herds which once covered the plains of the American West in numbers up to 60 million, made their last stand in Yellowstone. After a few short years of killing the animals for sport, for their hides, and ultimately as a means of controlling the Indians, perhaps as few as 23 bison survived in the wild in the United States.

Though Yellowstone had been established as a national park, there were no laws or personnel authorized to protect it. In the early years of the park, vandalism and poaching increased at such an alarming rate that finally, in 1886, the Army was sent to save the park from further destruction. In the winter of 1894, a poacher learned of the herd's location in the Pelican Valley and began to destroy them, one by one. Two soldiers were dispatched to the dangerous scene. They made a daring rush across a snowy landscape and managed to arrest the heavily armed man. The nation's last wild bison had been preserved.

Due to the public outcry surrounding this incident, Congress passed the Lacey Act in only 13 days to prohibit hunting in the national parks. Only because the area was remote, the animal well adapted to survive, and people committed to care,

are there bison in the wild today. So every time we see a buffalo in Yellowstone, it's cause for celebration of the national park idea—celebration of an animal's will to survive and of the human compassion to protect it.

WHERE ARE THE BEARS?

By far, the most famous player on the Yellowstone stage is the bear. Celebrated in cartoons and comic strips, the most well-known caricatures of the park's black bears are Yogi and Boo Boo of Jellystone Park. As endearing and memorable as they may be, this is not an image befitting a wild animal—and yet it characterizes the early days of resource management in Yellowstone. Instead of foraging along the forest's edge for grasses, roots, berries, and insects, black bears, like most species, are opportunistic, and were easily lured to the large garbage dumps near the park's hotels. Eventually, amphitheaters were built around the dumps so people could view the bears in comfort with a ranger standing guard nearby. Many visitors also remember black bears feeding from car windows along the roadside. What people don't remember is the average of 48 human injuries and the considerable property damage caused each year by these nuisance bears. Nor do they recall the many bears that had to be destroyed over the years as a result of this unnatural relationship with people.

More conflicts between people and grizzlies have occurred at Fishing Bridge than any other part of the park. Due to this high incidence of human injury and property damage, many of the visitor facilities have been removed from the area so that grizzlies may continue to use this stretch of lakeshore as a travel corridor between spawning streams. Color is not a reliable characteristic to differentiate between black bears and grizzlies, since both can vary in color from blonde to black. Grizzlies tend to be larger and have a distinguishable hump on their shoulders.

When the National Park Service was established in 1916, it was given a strong, but sometimes conflicting mission:

> *...to conserve the scenery and the natural and historic objects and the wildlife therein and to provide for the enjoyment of the same in such a manner and by such means as will leave them unimpaired for the enjoyment of future generations.*

Providing for too much "enjoyment" of a resource may just destroy what made it worth "conserving" in the first place. Into this confusion fell the bear. Managing bears simply for human enjoyment was destroying them. In the late 1960s and early 1970s, the dumps were closed and the feeding of bears from the roadside prohibited. Now, when people see a bear in Yellowstone, though less frequently than in the past, it is a rare and real experience of a bear as it should be, wild and free.

The Era of the Elk

The first snows of fall land on the back of the bull elk, who stretches his head forward to bugle, sending a challenge to other males and signaling the beginning of this annual ritual. This majestic animal, the American elk or *wapiti*, also presented a major challenge to the National Park Service's management of the natural resources under its care.

For several decades through the 1960s, park managers felt that only human control could keep the elk population down to a manageable size. During that period, an average of 1,000 elk were shot each year. With the advent of television, the killing of elk in Yellowstone became unacceptable to the American public. A special advisory board was convened to review the situation. At the completion of their study, they issued one of the most influential statements in the history of resource management.

They stated that the park should strive to preserve natural communities rather than specific species—preserving the whole, not just the individual parts. It also stated that park managers should reverse the changes that had been made, and restore what had been lost, to recreate where possible "a reasonable illusion of primitive America." This philosophy became known as natural regulation and it has guided wildlife management efforts throughout the National Park System ever since. It seemed there was

The Rocky Mountain elk or wapiti is the most abundant ungulate (hooved animal) in Yellowstone. The eerie high-pitched bugle of the bull elk fills the crisp fall air. Males will charge each other, occasionally locking antlers in battles for the groups of females, called "harems." This sparring action can often be seen on the grassy lawns in front of Fort Yellowstone.

CRAIG BLACKLOCK/LARRY ULRICH STOCK

much to learn from the notion of restoring all the parts of a natural system and then allowing nature to manage its own affairs.

On January 12, 1995, the National Park Service did just that. That historic morning, after over half a century of absence, gray wolves returned to Yellowstone. They were brought down from Canada, through the Roosevelt Arch into the park—a symbolic and triumphal return for an exiled species. Wolves had been hunted to extinction under an earlier, now seen as misguided policy, to remove all predators such as wolves, mountain lions, and coyotes, so that the prey species, especially the elk and deer populations, would grow. Today, wolves are thriving in the park's grassy valleys, and all the pieces of the Yellowstone puzzle are once again in place.

THE THREATENED GRIZZLY

Even though roughly 2.2 million acres are preserved within Yellowstone National Park, sometimes this is not enough to fulfill the mission of protecting the park's resources. Animals do not recognize political boundaries and may move outside the park, where attitudes toward them can be very different. This becomes especially serious when the survival of a resource is already in question. The grizzly bear is such a species. Officially regarded as "threatened" on the Endangered Species List, the territory needed to sustain a vi-

able population of these great bears extends well beyond the park. Yellowstone is the core of what is known as the Greater Yellowstone Ecosystem—an 18-million-acre area comprised of Yellowstone and Grand Teton national parks, seven national forests, three national wildlife refuges, and many private lands. Common ground must be found amongst all agencies and landowners if the bear is to survive in Yellowstone for future generations.

A huge effort has been made in the past several decades to increase the bear's chance of survival. This has included closing certain areas of critical habitat during the time the bears need them most, careful monitoring of human food storage, and a major public education program. Today, with the success of these efforts and coordination with agencies surrounding Yellowstone, park managers are cautiously optimistic about the future of grizzly bears in the Yellowstone Ecosystem. The grizzly bear represents for many that which is truly wild, and the human desire to preserve it.

We have seen how the national park idea has evolved from protecting things, to protecting natural communities, to protecting processes, to protecting ecosystems. Perhaps the human mind can evolve to a place where it can accept our last wild places on their own terms, even if these natural processes are beyond our control...such as fire.

FRANK S. BALTHIS

JEFF FOOTT

CAROL POLICH

The National Park Service aims to preserve all the original components of a natural ecosystem. Therefore, since wolves were eradicated over half a century ago, they have recently been reintroduced into Yellowstone and are doing quite well. Coyotes have had to readjust to the presence of this returning predator, and this has proven to be quite a challenge to them. Prey species, too, particularly the elk, have been surprised by this new carnivore on the scene. The park does not manage for specific population sizes, choosing instead to put all the players back into place and let the dynamics unfold as they will. Since coyotes in Yellowstone are notably big, especially with their winter coats of fur, people often confuse them for wolves. Though they are both in the dog family, they are different species. Wolves are twice as large as coyotes, standing three feet tall at the shoulder. Once one has seen a wolf, it is hard to make the same mistake again. Wolves have long legs and huge paws which appear almost out of proportion relative to their body size. Their faces are bulky and "German-shepherd" like.

Compared to wolves, a coyote's face is more delicate, with a notably narrower snout.

SUGGESTED READING

MCENEANEY, TERRY. *Birds of Yellowstone.* Boulder, Colorado: Roberts Rinehart, Inc. Publishers, 1988.

PHILLIPS, MICHAEL K. and DOUGLAS W. SMITH. *The Wolves of Yellowstone.* Stillwater, Minnesota: Voyageur Press, Inc., 1996.

ROBINSON, SANDRA C. and GEORGE B. *in pictures Yellowstone: The Continuing Story.* Las Vegas, Nevada: KC Publications, 1990.

SAMPLE, MICHAEL S. *Bison: Symbol of the American West.* Billings and Helena, Montana: Falcon Press Publishing Company, Inc., 1987.

SCHULLERY, PAUL. *The Bears of Yellowstone.* Worland, Wyoming: High Plains Publishing Company, Inc., 1992.

SCHULLERY, PAUL. *Searching for Yellowstone: Ecology and Wonder in the Last Wilderness.* New York, New York: Houghton Mifflin Co., 1997.

STREUBEL, DONALD. *Small Mammals of the Yellowstone Ecosystem.* Boulder, Colorado: Roberts Rinehart, Inc. Publishers, 1989.

VARLEY, JOHN D. and PAUL SCHULLERY. *Freshwater Wilderness: Yellowstone Fishes & Their World.* Yellowstone National Park, Wyoming: The Yellowstone Library and Museum Association, 1983.

WILKINSON, TODD. *Yellowstone Wildlife: A Watcher's Guide.* Minocqua, Wisconsin: NorthWord Press, Inc., 1992.

From Flames
–to Flowers

JEFF FOOTT

August 20, 1988. More acres burned on this day alone than in all of the previous years of Yellowstone's recorded history combined. Firefighters called it "Black Saturday." It was a climax in a seemingly surreal set of circumstances that surrounded this summer of fire.

Though it is well documented that major fires have occurred in Yellowstone once every several centuries, this season of flames still seemed to come as a surprise. Rainfall in April was 155 percent of normal and in May, 181 percent. The more likely prediction would have been that this would

be an abnormally wet year. What couldn't have been predicted was that it wouldn't rain virtually the entire summer, rather than several times a week, as is typical in Yellowstone. What started as an unusually wet spring became the driest summer on record. This drought, with an unprecedented number of lightning strikes and relentlessly high winds, combined to cause the conflagration of 1988.

Over 50 individual blazes reaching all corners of the park and beyond, eventually swirled into several large "complexes," or groups of fires. A few were human caused, while most were naturally ignited by lightning. The park's policy was to fight all human-caused fires, allowing natural fires to burn unless they threatened human life and property, recognizing the important role of fire in a forest ecosystem. Therefore, the natural fires that started in June and early July were allowed to burn. At the time, it looked as if they would do what most fires have done throughout the park's history, which is to go out after burning less than

ROGER J. ANDERSON

A wall of smoke and fire approaches the road before descending on the geyser basin at West Thumb. While a road normally serves as a firebreak to slow down a fire in a lodgepole forest, these flames merely hesitated for a moment and then rushed up the other side. In 1988, fire behaved in ways that even the most experienced firefighters had never seen before.

The large swath of burned trees surrounding the Old Faithful complex speaks of the heroic efforts made to save the historic buildings from the firestorm that swept through on September 7, 1988. Even at the climax of this event, however, the geysers continued to erupt, powered by forces of heat deep within the earth, completely undeterred by the flames at the surface.

an acre by running into a river, a lake, or a rainstorm. A fire that started in May in Lamar Valley had done just that. However, by July 15th, it was clear that this was a year like none other on record. With less than one percent of the park on fire, the decision was made from this day on, to fight all fires from their onset.

Campgrounds transformed into fire camps as, in the course of the summer, 25,000 personnel including several thousand military troops, and convoys of fire engines, helicopters, and planes came from all over the country. It was the largest firefighting effort in the history of the nation, and it succeeded only in protecting the buildings in the park. In the end, the fires were brought under control only after a quarter-inch of snow fell on September 11. What nature began, it also ended. The fires were officially declared out by mid-November.

When the smoke cleared, 36 percent of the park had burned and about 1 percent of the large mammals had perished. Several cabins at Old

DIANA L. STRATTON

A fire releases many nutrients into the soil. From this enriched earth sprouts a kaleidoscope of wildflowers, covering the blackened hillsides with color. Some, like the pink fireweed, grow only after fires have burned through an area.

Faithful were lost to the flames. Throughout the summer, television broadcasters announced the demise of the world's first national park. Newspaper headlines and editorials blazed about the park's failed fire policy.

What they failed to understand was the policy that nature itself had made—that the lodgepole forests that dominate the Yellowstone landscape are meant to burn at an interval of every 200 to 400 years, and that some lodgepole pine cones require the intense heat of fire to open their cones and release their seeds. What was it that created these dense green forests that people remember with such fondness? It was a catastrophic fire, much like this one, some 300 years ago.

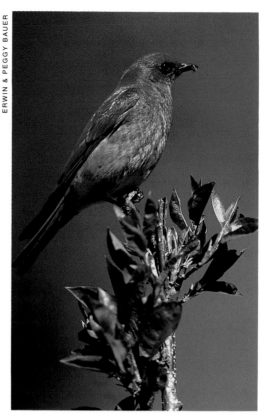

ERWIN & PEGGY BAUER

Mountain bluebirds nest primarily in dead trees and took advantage of the great opportunity afforded by the fires of 1988.

ED COOPER

The great writer Mark Twain once mused, "The reports of my death are greatly exaggerated." This was also true of Yellowstone. Within days, new grasses began to sprout up through the ash. Adapted to fire, nature reseeds itself in grand style. In some areas, lodgepoles dropped up to a million seeds per acre. In the succeeding summers, hillsides were covered with a brilliant array of wildflowers—pink fireweed, purple lupine, and yellow heart-leafed arnica. Aspen tree growth flourished. Dense mats of emerging lodgepole pine seedlings covered burned areas as thick as grass. Elk, bison, and other animals feasted on the acres of new browse which had been shaded out for centuries by the old-age forest. Birds which nest in the trunks of burned trees, such as woodpeckers, tree swallows, and mountain bluebirds, increased dramatically in number.

Visitors often ask if the National Park Service seeded any of the burned areas. It appears that nature did not need any help in this effort. The intense heat of the fires opened up the serotinous or fire-dependent cones which then dropped their seeds onto the open forest floor. These thickets of young lodgepoles are the next generation of the Yellowstone forest.

DIANA L. STRATTON

MARK & JENNIFER MILLER

Raptors, or birds of prey, including eagles, hawks, and the great gray owl, benefited from the burning of the ground cover, which exposed many rodents and other small animals immediately after the fires.

The burning of much of the tree canopy opened up the forest floor to sunlight, resulting in acres of new browse for Yellowstone's grazing animals.

ED COOPER

The fires created a greater variety of habitat for birds. The yellow-headed blackbird prefers marshy areas and was little affected by the fires.

All in all, the fires created a richer, more diverse habitat for wildlife. 1988 was a turning point in the natural history of Yellowstone.

Still, change is often hard for people to understand, particularly when the park will not look the same in our lifetime. The fires of 1988 provide us an opportunity to look beyond ourselves to changes that will benefit future generations as well as species other than our own. And while fire may not be pretty in some people's eyes, it is natural—and that, in the end, is what the parks are intended to preserve.

Former park chief naturalist George Robinson once noted that fire is not the final curtain on the stage that is Yellowstone. It is the opening act of a drama that will play over and over again until the end of time.

SUGGESTED READING AND VIDEOS

DE GOLIA, JACK. *Fire: A Force of Nature*. Las Vegas, Nevada: KC Publications, Inc., 1989.

EKEY, BOB et al. *Yellowstone On Fire*. Billings, Montana: The Billings Gazette, 1995.

SHAW, RICHARD J. *Plants of Yellowstone National Park and Grand Teton National Park*. Salt Lake City: Wheelwright Press, Ltd., 1981.

Yellowstone—The Unfinished Story: The Fires of Yellowstone and the Park's Natural Recovery. A National Park Service Production. Huron, South Dakota: Landis-Trailwood Films.

Yesterday's Yellowstone

People have long been drawn to Yellowstone. As early as 10,000 years ago, they found their way to this mysterious land, and even today, native people return for ceremonies and other spiritual purposes. Only one group of Indians—a band of Shoshone—was known to actually live in Yellowstone year round. Known as the Sheepeaters, they devised clever strategies to hunt the bighorn sheep, which included the use of bows they fashioned masterfully from the horn of the ram. It is unknown why they never obtained the horse or the gun as other native cultures did. Maybe they were not in a position to trade for these technologies, or perhaps they chose instead to embrace their traditional ways. Reports from some of the first mountain men to meet them say only that they were a peaceful and generous people.

But while Yellowstone was home to only a few, it was a crossroads for many. The Crow, Blackfeet, Flathead, and Bannock people, among others, came to this high mountain plateau to follow the buffalo which was for them, in many ways, a source of life. Yellowstone's obsidian, a black volcanic glass, was highly sought after for making tools and weapons and was traded among native people all across the continent. So, long before it was set aside as a park, Yellowstone was already a place of national significance.

Even the name of the park speaks of its Native American origins. It is thought that when the French-Canadian fur traders encountered the Minnataree Indians in what is today eastern Montana, they inquired about the name of the

The Lower Falls and the Canyon have much the same impact on visitors today as they did on explorer Charles Cook. Upon first seeing the canyon, he wrote, "I sat there in amazement while my companions came up, and after that, it seemed to me that it was five minutes before anyone spoke."

RUSS FINLEY

LARRY ULRICH

With less snow and warmer temperatures, thermal areas are a sanctuary for wildlife in winter. When John Colter arrived in Yellowstone on foot in the winter of 1807-08, he encountered a scene much like this. Prior to Colter, the land had been traversed only by Native Americans, who sought out the region for bison and other resources.

ART WOLFE

The culture of Yellowstone's only resident native people revolved around the bighorn sheep.

river that flows into the Missouri there. The Indians referred to the yellow sandstone bluffs through which this river flows and called it *Mi tse a-da-zi*, which means "yellow rock" or "yellow stone." It is this same river, which begins its long journey far away in the park, that gives it its name.

Fifty years before the establishment of Yellowstone, landscape painter George Catlin had an earlier notion of what a national park could be. As the nation's frontier was beginning to disappear, he proposed that the entire area west of the Mississippi River be set aside to protect the land and the culture of its native people. He called it "a nation's park containing man and beast...preserved in their primitive beauty and wildness, where the world could see for ages to come, the Native Indian." But Catlin's idea did not come to pass.

The park's original inhabitants left for reservations in 1871. Yet still today, when we stand at Obsidian Cliff where they quarried its rocks, or at Sheepeater Cliffs where they hunted the bighorn, it is as though their spirit is still here.

TALES OF THE TRAPPERS

The famous Lewis and Clark Expedition never saw Yellowstone. Though they had heard of these uncharted lands from local Indians, their travels took them just north of the region. One of their scouts, however, asked to be discharged from the party to go and explore them. This man, John Colter, is considered to be the first white

ED COOPER

This grand stone archway welcomes visitors into the park through its north entrance today, just as it did in the early days of the park when President Theodore Roosevelt dedicated it in 1903 "for the benefit and enjoyment of the people."

ney home. Of this day in 1870, Nathaniel Langford wrote in his journal:

> *We had within a distance of 50 miles, seen what we believed to be the greatest wonders on the continent.... Judge then, of our astonishment on entering this basin, to see at no great distance before us, an immense body of sparkling water, projected suddenly and with terrific force into the air to a height of over one hundred feet. We had found a real geyser. In the valley before us were a thousand hot springs of various sizes and character.... We gave such names to those of the geysers which we saw in action as we think will best illustrate their peculiarities. The one I have just described, General Washburn has named "Old Faithful", because of the regularity of its eruption.*

Though Langford represented the Northern Pacific Railroad, which had obvious interests in attracting people to the area, he later became a powerful proponent of the national park idea. His lectures caught the attention of others, including the nation's chief geologist, Dr. Ferdinand Hayden, who persuaded Congress of the need for an official fact-finding tour of this little-known land. The Hayden Survey included photographer William Henry Jackson and painter Thomas Moran, whose works would magnificently document the natural curiosities of Yellowstone for all the world to see. Hayden wrote of this incomparable place in this way:

> *The intelligent American will one day point on the map to this remarkable district with the conscious pride that it has not its parallel on the face of the globe.*

THE WORLD'S FIRST NATIONAL PARK

After efforts by several members of these expeditions and by railroad interests, President Ulysses S. Grant signed the bill establishing Yellowstone as the world's first national park in 1872. The legislation passed easily, because Congress was persuaded that this land was

person to enter the Yellowstone. He was planning to trap beaver, whose pelts were a valuable commodity since they were a fashion rage in Europe. He and other trappers, including Jim Bridger and Joe Meek, established trade relations with the Indians and also drafted some of the earliest maps of the area. But few people believed the stories they told of the strange things they'd seen.

Bridger told stories of fountains of water shooting hundreds of feet into the air and of a hot spring along the lakeshore where a person could catch a fish and then cook it while pulling it up through the boiling water. He spoke of "...peetrified trees a-growing, with peetrified birds on 'em a-singing peetrified songs."

EXPEDITION: YELLOWSTONE

The wild tales of the trappers, however, stirred the imagination of the nation. Three major expeditions set forth to find the facts for themselves. The Folsom-Peterson-Cook Expedition of 1869 substantiated the wonders of the region, inspiring others to follow. After weeks of difficult travel, having explored the Canyon, the Mud Volcano, the Lake, and the West Thumb, the Washburn Expedition, convinced they'd seen all there was to see, headed north over the Continental Divide on their jour-

RANDI HIRSCHMANN

*True to its name,
Old Faithful Geyser
still erupts as
regularly to the
delight of visitors as
it did when the
Washburn Expedition
named it in 1870.
The great geyser's
average interval
has changed
a little throughout
the history of
the park, but
the eruptions are
as faithful as
ever. It was primarily
for the geysers
and other geologic
wonders that
Yellowstone was
established as
the world's first
national park.*

worthless for any economic purposes such as timber, agriculture, and mining. They would probably never have guessed that this rather obscure bill contained an idea that would one day become the pride of the nation. Today, there are over 370 units of the U. S. National Park System, and many other parks and protected areas in over 140 countries around the world.

GUARDIANS OF THE PARKS

It seems that the stroke of a pen in Washington does not necessarily ensure the protection of resources thousands of miles away. Back in Yellowstone, wildlife continued to be poached, trees harvested, and thermal features vandalized with devastating results. In response, the United States Army was called to the park's rescue in 1886. For 32 years, in a most unusual assignment, the Cavalry protected the park with military precision. With time, however, the officers in charge of Yellowstone became increasingly aware that the role of the military was to protect national security, not natural resources.

By the early 1900s, several more national parks had been established—Sequoia, General Grant (now King's Canyon), Yosemite, Mount Rainier, and Crater Lake. These fledgling new parks were managed by different means. Some were afforded military protection, while others were under civilian administration. By 1914, the need was obvious for a unified civilian approach to managing the fragmented park system. The National Park Service was created in 1916 and its park rangers became the new guardians of the Yellowstone, preserving it with the proud legacy left to them by the Army.

Soldier stations like this one at Norris were built throughout the park by the Army. This building is now a museum chronicling the story of soldiers, scouts, and the rangers who are today's guardians of the parks.

THEY CALLED IT "WONDERLAND"

An early visit to Yellowstone was a true challenge. Arriving by train near the park entrance, visitors boarded stagecoaches pulled by teams of six horses to begin their adventure "on the grand tour."

To see the sights of the park, they endured rutted roads and the outlandish stories of their drivers along the way. Occasionally, the horses could not pull the weight of the stagecoach up the steep hills. Passengers were obliged to get out and walk, or help push the coach up the grade. Some became victims of stagecoach holdups. The robbers were more greedy than dangerous, however, and most visitors decided that it was just another part of the Yellowstone experience.

Eventually they arrived, covered with dust, at their destination for the evening. The "dudes," people of means who could afford the expense of hotel stays, dined in elegance at the park's few grand hotels such as the Lake Hotel and the Old Faithful Inn. The "sagebrushers," those staying at the established tent camps or camping with their own makeshift gear, gathered around a blazing fire, telling stories, singing songs, eating popcorn, and anticipating the possible visit of a mischievous bear. However rigorous the day might have been, visitors were enchanted by the park's many curiosities. They called it "Wonderland."

Fort Yellowstone represents the proud legacy left by the military after their 32-year administration of the park. Scottish stone masons built the sturdy sandstone structures of Officers' Row. This building, formerly the bachelor officers' quarters, serves as the Visitor Center today, named for the park's first civilian superintendent and one of the founders of the National Park Service, Horace M. Albright.

RUSS FINLEY

The Old Faithful Inn was built during the winter of 1903-04. Its extraordinary log design was intended by architect Robert Reamer to bring the outside in, and reflect in a man-made structure, the beauty of nature itself. It is an excellent example of a style which became known as "rustic architecture" or "parkitecture" and has charmed visitors throughout the decades.

JEFF & ALEXA HENRY

Built in the early 1920s, Lake Ranger Station was one of a series of buildings constructed for the new park rangers as they took over management of the park from the military.

Ranger naturalists like Mike Arthur continue the legacy of early soldiers and rangers interpreting the mysteries and messages of Yellowstone for park visitors. As Superintendent Horace Albright wrote, "Rangers should be interpreters of the mountains, their moods and mysteries. They should serve as philosopher, guide, and friend." Join a ranger today for a walk along park trails or a talk around the campfire at amphitheaters throughout the park. Be a part of the tradition of Yellowstone.

JEFF & ALEXA HENRY

Like the first people to encounter Yellowstone, visitors today experience a land of mysteries.

RUSS FINLEY

YELLOWSTONE TODAY

While a visit to Yellowstone today is not as arduous as in the past, it can be every bit as full of wonder. It behooves us to ponder for a moment, as we walk upon this famous land, what the national park idea means to each of us.

Perhaps it is in the national parks where we begin to understand our role in the grand scheme of nature. As one writer has written about Rocky Mountain National Park:

> *Of all the reasons we have to get away from it all and to escape to these mountains from time to time, perhaps the one that is the most compelling is an unconscious reason. We sense that somehow our roots as human beings are nestled into the floor of these forests....We are from this wilderness, and we return in our yearning to know our history....For even though our wilder origins have, for the most part, been acculturated out of us, there remains a strong unconscious memory of our connectedness with the earth. We return for mysterious and unspoken reasons, as if on a pilgrimage to a sacred place.*
>
> *-Paul Firnhaber*

Or maybe it's as simple as naturalist John Muir wrote, that "we need beauty as well as bread, places to play in as well as to pray in, where nature may heal..."

SUGGESTED READING AND VIDEOS

ALBRIGHT, HORACE M. and FRANK J. TAYLOR, *Oh, Ranger! A Book About the National Parks*. Golden, Colorado: Outbooks, Inc., 1980.

CLARY, DAVID A. *The Place Where Hell Bubbled Up: A History of the First National Park*. Moose, Wyoming: Homestead Publishing, 1993.

HAINES, AUBREY L. *The Yellowstone Story: Volumes I & II*. Niwot, Colorado: University Press of Colorado, 1996.

LANGFORD, NATHANIEL PITT. *The Discovery of Yellowstone Park: Journal of the Washburn Expedition to the Yellowstone and Firehole Rivers in the Year 1870*. Lincoln, Nebraska: University of Nebraska Press, 1972.

MILSTEIN, MICHAEL. *Yellowstone: 125 Years of America's Best Idea*. Billings, Montana: The Billings Gazette, 1996.

MUIR, JOHN. *The Yellowstone National Park*. Golden, Colorado: Outbooks, 1986.

The Challenge of Yellowstone. Harper's Ferry, West Virginia: Harper's Ferry History Association, Inc.

Yellowstone: The First National Park. The Reader's Digest Association, Inc., San Ramon, California: International Video Network, 1988.

Maybe some of us come to the national parks to remember what beauty is. Watching the sun set over the mountains, we may remember that one of Nature's gifts is peace. Here is a sanctuary for the soul, where we can come to be refreshed and renewed.

Perhaps in the end, we're drawn to this place because we're proud of it. We may recall the story about the campfire around which the Washburn Expedition talked and allegedly went beyond their own private gain to propose a park for the benefit of all. Ironically, while the land was set aside, to some degree, because it was perceived to have no mineral or other economic value, it has come to represent a notion invaluable to the people of this nation. Though historians may not agree on exactly when and where it happened, the legend endures that it was in Yellowstone that the national park idea was born.

Here a nation sent a strong message to the rest of the world—that there is untold value in wildness, and that it is ever important to preserve our vanishing wilderness, the wildlife that depends on it, and the natural processes that keep it wild.

RUSS FINLEY

The national park idea attributes value to wildlife and wildlands.

KC Publications has been the leading publisher of colorful, interpretive books about National Park areas, public lands, Indian lands, and related subjects for over 39 years. We have 6 active series—over 125 titles—with Translation Packages in up to 8 languages for over half the areas we cover. Write, call, or visit our web site for our full-color catalog.

Our series are:

The Story Behind the Scenery® – Compelling stories of over 65 National Park areas and similar Public Land areas. Some with Translation Packages.

in pictures... The Continuing Story® – A companion, pictorially oriented, series on America's National Parks. All titles have Translation Packages.

For Young Adventurers™ – Dedicated to young seekers and keepers of all things wild and sacred. Explore America's Heritage from A to Z.

Voyage of Discovery® – Exploration of the expansion of the western United States.

Indian Culture and the Southwest – All about Native Americans, past and present.

Calendars – For National Parks and Southwest Indian culture, in dramatic full color, and a companion Color Your Own series, with crayons.

To receive our full-color catalog featuring over 125 titles—Books, Calendars, Screen Scenes, Videos, Audio Tapes, and other related specialty products:

Call (800-626-9673), fax (702-433-3420), write to the address below, Or visit our web site at www.kcpublications.com

Published by KC Publications, 3245 E. Patrick Ln., Suite A, Las Vegas, NV 89120.

Inside Back Cover: Yellowstone preserves the bison—symbol of wild America. Photo by Adam Jones.

Back Cover: In places like Mammoth Hot Springs, Yellowstone preserves that which is rare and beautiful. Photo by Larry Ulrich.

Created, Designed, and Published in the U.S.A.
Printed by Tien Wah Press (Pte.) Ltd, Singapore

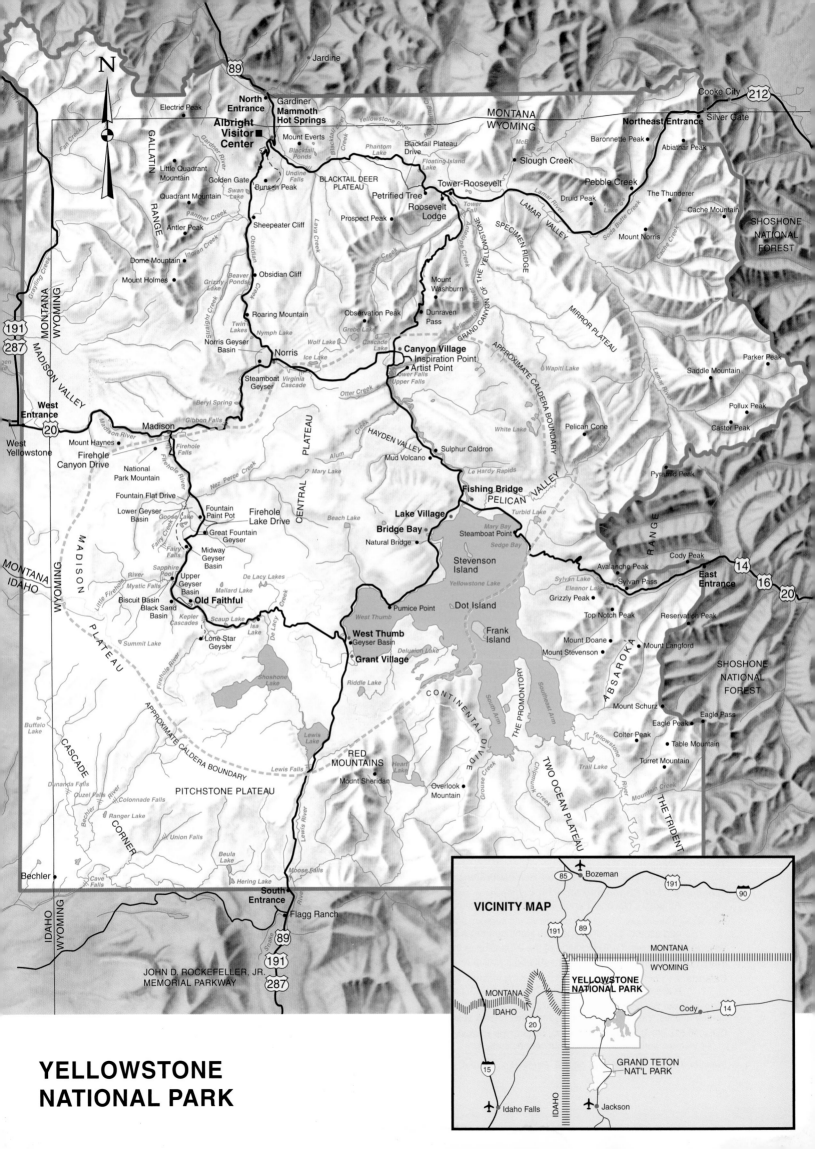

YELLOWSTONE
NATIONAL PARK

VICINITY MAP